Little Pebble™

Our Families

Mothers
Are Part of a Family

by Lucia Raatma

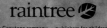

raintree

a Capstone company — publishers for children

Raintree is an imprint of Capstone Global Library Limited, a company incorporated in England and Wales having its registered office at 264 Banbury Road, Oxford, OX2 7DY – Registered company number: 6695582

www.raintree.co.uk
myorders@raintree.co.uk

ISBN 978 1 4747 4570 3
21 20 19 18 17
10 9 8 7 6 5 4 3 2 1

British Library Cataloguing in Publication Data
A full catalogue record for this book is available from the British Library.

Editorial Credits
Christianne Jones, editor; Juliette Peters, designer;
Wanda Winch, media researcher; Laura Manthe, production specialist

Photo Credits
Capstone Studio: Karon Dubke, 5, 7, 9, 13, 15, 19, 21; Shutterstock: Angelina Babii, paper texture, Dubova, 17, Monkey Business Images, cover, Photographee.eu, 11, Syda Productions, 1, Teguh Mujiono, tree design

Contents

Mothers

A mother has children.

She is a parent.

Some mothers are called mum. Some are called mama.

What mothers do

Cam plays piano.

His mum helps.

Rayan's mum works in an office. She is busy.

Luca's mum builds houses.

She works hard.

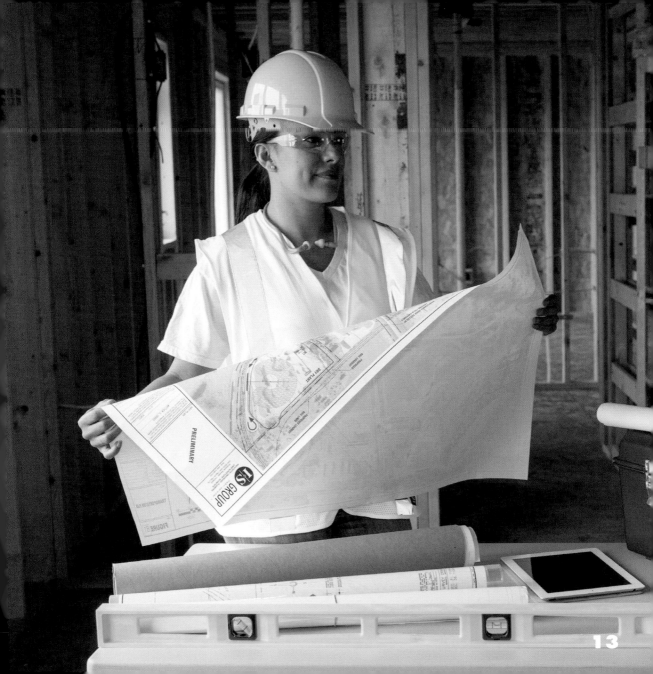

Thomas and his mum
bake. They love cookies!

Ava's mums like to be outside. Ava does too.

Anna feels sick. Her mum gives her medicine.

Mothers snuggle.

Mothers kiss.

Mothers love.

Glossary

bake – to cook in an oven

mama – another name for mum

medicine – a pill or treatment for healing an illness

office – a place where people go to work

parent – a mother or father

snuggle – to hold close

Find out more

Family (Say What You See), Rebecca Rissman (Raintree, 2014)

My Mum (Family World), Caryn Jenner (Franklin Watts, 2013)

Who's in My Family?: All About Our Families (Let's Talk about You and Me), Robie H Harris (Candlewick Press, 2012)

Websites

https://www.activityvillage.co.uk/british-royal-family
Use printables, colouring pages, posters, worksheets and learn-to-draw activities to learn more about the British Royal Family.

https://www.activityvillage.co.uk/family
Download and print out cards, colouring sheets, and more information about families.

Index